SCHOOLS THEN AND NOW

Rachel Kranz

Contents

Rigby
A Harcourt Achieve Imprint

www.Rigby.com
1-800-531-5015

Long ago, some towns did not have many people living in them. All students could fit in one room. They went to school in a one-room schoolhouse.

Hello, my name is Abigail. This is my class from long ago.

Today towns have more people, which means more students. They have bigger schools and lots of classrooms.

Long ago, some children traveled many miles to get an education. They walked or rode in wagons.

Today some students still walk
to school.
Others ride to school in buses.

It's nice to meet you, too!

CLASSROOMS

Long ago, students of every grade sat in the same classroom. Older students sometimes helped younger students.

Today students in one classroom
are usually in the same grade.
Each classroom has its own teacher.

Long ago, schools had
very few supplies.
The whole school had only
one map and one blackboard.

Today we have more classrooms and many more supplies. Many classrooms have computers and lots of books.

Wow! Your classroom is really different.

LUNCH

Long ago, children carried
their lunch to school in pails.
In warm weather, they ate outside.
In cold weather, they ate
in the classroom.

Today many children carry lunch
to school in lunch bags.
Some schools have cafeterias
where you can buy your lunch.

Long ago, everyone helped take care of the school. Children helped with jobs like building fires and pumping water.

That looks like my rabbit. I could do that job!

Today children still have jobs. They might pass out supplies or take care of a class pet.

MUSIC AND ART

Long ago, music and art were taught in the regular classroom. Students liked painting pictures and playing instruments.

Today students still enjoy
music and art.
Sometimes these subjects
are taught in special rooms.

Many things have changed,
but some have stayed the same.
School is still a place to learn,
play, and make lots of friends.